Following the Snow Leopard

Following the Snow Leopard

Poems by

Barbara Wiedemann

© 2025 Barbara Wiedemann. All rights reserved.
This material may not be reproduced in any form, published,
reprinted, recorded, performed, broadcast,
rewritten or redistributed without
the explicit permission of Barbara Wiedemann.
All such actions are strictly prohibited by law.

Cover design by Shay Culligan
Cover image by Barbara Wiedemann
Author photo by Winnie Roberts

ISBN: 978-1-63980-801-4

Kelsay Books
502 South 1040 East, A-119
American Fork, Utah 84003
Kelsaybooks.com

for Nichole and Matt and Winnie and Thurston

Acknowledgments

The following poems, sometimes in different versions, have apeared in these publications:

Acorn: "Fly Fishing"
Alpha Beat Soup: "Morning Coffee"
American Whitewater: "Antidote to Urban Living"
Blueline: "The View from the Taller Mountain"
California Quarterly::"On Seeing Eternity in the Distance"
Di-verse-city: "The Exchange"
John Clare Society Newsletter: "Afternoon Visit to a Smaller World," "The Beauty of Indirection," "Homage to Beauty, "Sixth Extinction," "Written Near Mammoth, California"
Kerf: "Canyon Country," "Coyotes," "Desert Meditation," "Graffiti," "One Hundred Miles North of the Grand Canyon," "Sunset at Burnt Ridge," "A Visitor to the Night World," "Where the Buffalo Roam"
Lalitamba: "Mountains and Pine Forests"
Laughing Dog: "Destination Unknown"
Paper Street: "Reassurance"
Red Owl: "Contemplating Time"
Red Rock Review: "April 27"
Southern Women's Review: "Following the Snow Leopard," "Magical Realism Comes to the Desert"

Some poems in this collection also appear in the chapbooks*:*

Desert Meditations (Finishing Line Press, 2018)
Half-Life of Love (Finishing Line Press, 2008)
Sometime in October (Finishing Line Press, 2010)

Contents

Following the Snow Leopard — 13
A Conversation with Myself — 14
The High Plains of Texas — 15
Coyotes — 16
Visiting Ghost Ranch — 18
The San Mateo Mountains of New Mexico — 19
Evil Jungle Princess — 20
Sounds of the Desert Near Rio Chama — 21
Desert Meditation — 22
Kelly, New Mexico — 23
Mary's Bar — 24
Sometime in October — 26
North of the Grand Canyon — 27
April 27 — 28
The Golden Years — 29
Graffiti — 30
Canyon Country — 31
The Exchange — 32
Thresholds — 33
Antidote to Urban Living — 34
What Emily Dickinson Knew — 35
An Afternoon Visit to a Smaller World — 36
The Trail to Heart Lake — 38
The Moment of Stillness — 40
Near the Bristlecone Pine Forest — 41
Hiking the Pacific Crest Trail — 42
The View from the Taller Mountain — 43
Reassurance — 44
Written Near Mammoth, California — 45
Transcendence — 46
On Seeing Eternity in the Distance — 47

Contemplating Time	48
The Sixth Extinction	49
The Pelican Squadron (or Brief, Pod, Pouch)	50
The Flight of the Brown Pelicans	51
The Oregon Coast Near Langlois	52
Destination Unknown	54
The Unschooled Birdwatcher	55
The Rock Garden	56
Breathing the Wild	57
Mountains and Pine Forests	58
The Amplitude of the Earth	60
A Visitor to the Night World	61
Fly Fishing	62
The Rabbits of Coeur d'Alene	64
Sumptuous Solitude	66
The Butterflies of the Amazon	67
Ode to Cowboys	68
Vedauwoo, Wyoming	69
Where the Buffalo Roam	70
The Kennebec Pass Near Durango	71
The Beauty of Indirection	72
Magical Realism Comes to the Desert	73
Sunset at Burnt Ridge	74
Against Shale Oil Exploration in the Desert	76
Homage to Beauty	77
The Dance of the Elk	78
Another Dance	79
Requiem for the Bees	80
Once Upon a Time	82
Losing Paradise	84
Mountains and Trees and Caterpillars	86

Our Legacy	88
In the Footsteps of the Dinosaurs	89
Out of the Ashes Emerge Saplings	90
Finding the Magic	92

Following the Snow Leopard

"No one has explained what the leopard was seeking at that altitude."
 —Ernest Hemingway, epigraph of "The Snows of Kilimanjaro"

Living in a small western town
shadowed by a mountain
she's caught up in mundane tasks
grocery shopping, laundry,
social chitchat
but when she lifts her eyes
away from the ordinary
there the mountain
a jagged peak of snow and rock
is still in sunlight
and she knows
that's where she's going,
where she must go.
All she has to do
is follow the trail out of town.

A Conversation with Myself

I have to—
I will.
      "Do you think you can?"
I guess.

The High Plains of Texas

The oil industry has brought changes to many Texas towns. Needmore no longer needs more. There is evidence of prosperity, but perhaps there are losses as well.

About as far west as you can go
in the Texas Panhandle
are towns with names like
Muleshoe, Circleback, and Needmore,
names that tell a history.

Needmore I drive through—
a few houses, no stores or a gas station
an abandoned co-op gin—
Needmore perhaps needs more.

But on the other hand
you would have your family, a few friends,
a livelihood from the fields of the high plains
and just south of town
one hundred thousand sand hill cranes
winter every year.

So, does anyone need more?

Coyotes

I heard the coyotes this morning,
first one, then another
maybe seven or eight in all.
My dog quieted
hearing a language
she couldn't quite understand.

As the sun rose,
we walked towards the cliffs,
     first desert grasses,
          then sage and cholla
               with fuchsia flowers
                    like crinkled tissue paper.

Near the cliffs, pines
with trunks cracked and twisted
suggesting age and struggle.
Juniper I know,
the others I can't name.

Then rising before us,
     layers of rose, cream, and gold
          carved by wind,
               rock so soft
                    my fingernail leaves its mark.

And at night, stars
        undimmed by any city lights,
                galaxies upon galaxies
                      uncountable.

At least once we should all hear the coyotes sing.

Visiting Ghost Ranch

to Georgia O'Keeffe

I have stood where you have,
        seen the rose—and gold-colored cliffs,
            smelled the sage and juniper,
                felt the dry desert air,
                      and heard the coyotes at dusk.

Now I understand your paintings,
        uncluttered and primal,
              reduced to the elements.

The San Mateo Mountains of New Mexico

The San Mateo Mountains
south of Albuquerque
are unadorned by trees
and over the millennia
have been etched
by wind and meager rainfall
exposing brown and red rocks
and carving gullies and canyons.

Pared down to the essentials
are these New Mexico mountains—
nothing extraneous.

Evil Jungle Princess

Maybe this is what she always wanted to be
maybe this is the image she sought

maybe this is to be her future
maybe this is who she already is
or maybe was.

So when she saw
Evil Jungle Princess
on the Thai menu she ordered it.

And she was not disappointed
with her plate of chicken,
straw mushrooms, lemon grass, and basil

even though the restaurant was in Taos,
the land of Mexican food.

Sounds of the Desert Near Rio Chama

So still the desert is
that you hear
the raven's wings against the air
    like a breath exhaling
        or maybe like the slow panting of an animal,
            a dog perhaps.

So quiet the desert is
that you sometimes hear sounds
    like the crackle and pop
        of a breakfast cereal
            emanate from the juniper and pinyon pines.

You must look closely
to discover the bark-colored locusts
    snapping and rubbing
        their gossamer wings together.

So still and quiet the desert is
that you find yourself again.

Desert Meditation

Have you ever watched
      rain in a desert,
            the first drops
                  before the ground is moist?

The earth releases
      a small puff of dust
          as each drop
                impacts the ground.

Kelly, New Mexico

Bits of broken glass
are scattered among
the old stone foundations,
not today's glass,
transparent and clear,
nor that of brown beer bottles,

but bits of green and aqua
weathered to opaqueness,
other shards with shades of lilac,
the color, a magical meeting of
manganese dioxide and sunlight,

some amber pieces
with markings that hint
of a use unknown,
and several of brown,
aged until they now shimmer
with opalescence in the sunlight.

Old glass
beautiful in its oldness
suggests stories
that have long been forgotten.

Mary's Bar

In Cerrillos,
a town of few people,
old adobe structures
and house trailers
border unpaved streets.
At the crossroads
stands Mary's Bar
with its old porch and door
weathered by the glaring New Mexico sun.

"You must go to the bar,"
the stranger had said in Socorro
one hundred miles to the south.
And so I did.

Inside
a wooden counter and stools
slowly emerge from the darkness.
And as if forgotten in an attic,
a tattered couch
a cast iron stove
an old red metal cooler
line the walls,
and stacks of yellowed newspapers
fill the corners.

Outside
two women
old enough to have forgotten youth
sit on the porch
lean toward each other
confide and giggle and drink their beers.

Sometime in October

Sometime in October
      we'll get together and talk
            reminisce about the spring and summer
                look at photographs
                      laugh about our foolishness
                            mourn the losses.

Sometime in October
      when the leaves have fallen
          and nature takes a rest
                when winter is imminent

we'll get together   and celebrate.

North of the Grand Canyon

So quiet
is this remote canyon
on the Kaibab Plateau
described as "desolate"
in the guidebooks,

so still
is this place called Snake Gulch
that I wake to the sounds
of my breathing,
nothing else.

It is too cool for insects,
too early for birds,
too soon for the sun
that will warm the canyon walls
causing breezes

that will disturb and thus rustle
the sage and grasses and juniper,
but now nothing,
only the sound
of my slow, easy breathing.

This is the silence
the Ancestral Pueblo
and later the Paiutes
would have known.

April 27

I left you at the bottom of the Canyon
along the steep rocky walls of a side ravine.
In the peacefulness of predawn
I placed your photograph
among red and black rocks two billion years old,
the Colorado River in view.

I left you
       with small flowers like buttercups
       with purple blossoms on a vine
       with pungent sage.

I left you
       with a grey bird the size of my thumb
       with a copper-tinted rattlesnake
       coiled precisely, waiting for the warming sun.

There I left you   and began the long hike out.

The Golden Years

There are
      fathers and grandfathers
      uncles and brothers
      lovers and friends
      and maybe a husband or two.
Sometimes they turn away   sometimes they die.

But eventually   you are there   alone,

      no one between you and the world

      and   the world   is   yours.

Graffiti

The visitor center at Moab
has a brochure about rock art
and about the creators of the petroglyphs—
the Barrier Canyon people, the Fremont,
the Ancestral Pueblo, and the Ute,
inhabitants of the region
from four thousand years ago
until the introduction of the horse.
The brochure maps out the sites
where one can view
the pecked, incised, and chiseled
desert varnish of the sandstone
where one can examine
the outlines of big horn sheep, antelopes,
elk and centipedes,
and birthing women and kachinas—
where one can ponder
the symbols for migration
and for the land and for the heavens.

The culture is written on the rock—
something like spray paint on abandoned buildings.

Canyon Country

Silvery lupine
spreading daisy
common paintbrush
in hues from pale orange to red
larkspur
desert phlox
scarlet gila
blue flax
and others unidentified
color the meadow.
And higher up
still blooming
on this day in early June
are blue irises
and soon will blossom
rock goldenrod.

And to think
        I once was content
                with the flower shop
                      on Main Street.

The Exchange

The pines of the West are many
and to me indistinguishable
but she told me a secret—
ponderosa pines
smell like vanilla.
The crevices of the bark
exude the rich textured scent
of vanilla.

The stranger gave me a gift
wanting nothing in return
but I offered her
the possibility of adventure
in my tales
of a woman alone
but for a dog.

Thresholds

The door is always there
      multiple doors really
           opening in all directions.

But most keep them closed
      often even locked
           afraid to venture out
                to move beyond the ordinary
                      into the unknown

but the possibility   is always there.

And once on the other side
      you wonder what took so long
           why you hesitated

and the next time   it is easier.

Antidote to Urban Living

The Middle Fork American River
from Greenwood Bridge site
to Mammoth Bar
flows deep in a ravine
but still is easy to kayak.

Paddlers enter into this canyon world
but few others breach its rock walls.
Undisturbed are deer at water's edge
a duck family in an eddy
and the raptors overhead.

Swimming in unison
two river otters
look at the kayaker
then dive, resurface
and look again.

Four more are stacked on a rock
warming in the sun.

Shouldn't we all just venture out?

What Emily Dickinson Knew

On the red brick patio
      is a large terra cotta pot
      imported from Italy
      planted with yellow chrysanthemums.

Hidden in the green leaves
      is a green chameleon
      motionless on a flower stalk

      or a tree branch   in a lizard world.

An Afternoon Visit to a Smaller World

The snake,
eighteen inches   pencil thin
gray and beige stripes,
fits itself into the slight crevice
of a gray and beige rock,
a foot or so from shore.
There it suns itself
joined by blue dragonflies.

Slowly the snake
s-curves onto a branch
gently swayed by wind waves.
There it waits and stares
into the region beneath the surface,
so still, flies crawl along its length.
Its orange tongue tastes the water
and by tasting senses prey,
or so it seems.

A golden shiner,
just a minnow really,
ventures near,
a sudden lunge   a miss
and the snake resumes its wait.
Finally unnourished
it curls back on itself
to regain its island home.

I continue my walk
along Castle Lake
and when I return
the snake is gone   at least to me.

The Trail to Heart Lake

Even the sixty-three hundred foot
Black Butte is insignificant
with Mt. Shasta to its right.
Snow-covered Mt. Shasta,
its silence only temporary,
deserves the legends
of those who honor it.
Watching or perhaps waiting,
I sit on granite
two hundred million years old,
a magma outcropping,
in an ancient sea bed.
Seven hundred feet below me
is Castle Lake,
left by a receding glacier,
the same that carved
Heart Lake behind me.

Into the lake I step
expecting the cold of melting snow
but its waters are cool silk
against my skin.
My clothes left on a rock await me,
my body soon to be warmed
by the sun and rock
and then to be chilled
by the breezes of the mountains,

the same breezes that blend
the scents of the blossoming shrubs
into one sweetness
on this first day of July

but still a spring day on the mountain
where the only sounds are the insects,
the birds' wings against the air,
and the wind moving through
the western white pine.

Should I taste the nectar
that attracts the bees
or the snow left in small patches?
Or are four senses pleasured enough?

The Moment of Stillness

The sound of the bird's wing
the color of the leaf

the smoothness of the manzanita bark
erase the problems

I have carried with me
on this mountain trail

until only this moment exists
and I am absorbed

by the distant mountains
and the near rocks.

Near the Bristlecone Pine Forest

"I wanted to hear the forbidden blood song."
—Caity Weaver, *NYT.* 11/23/2022

Near the bristlecone pines,
        the world's oldest living organisms,
        some around before the pyramids,
        I camp alone but for my dog.

When night falls and the wind lessens
        when the insects cease foraging
        and the birds still,
        silence reigns.

And then you hear your body
        your inhaling and exhaling
        your swallowing   your heart beating.

And if it's truly quiet, you hear something else,
        the sound of blood coursing
        through your arteries   your veins.
        the "forbidden blood song."

So very quiet it must be to hear this
        never in a city or town,
        never in our tech-driven life.

But after awhile you're grateful
        for the distant storm   the rising wind
        for the small unseen animal
        gnawing on something unknown.

You're grateful for life beyond yours.

Hiking the Pacific Crest Trail

These are gifts—

the lunar eclipse turning the moon red
that cold, cold night in the desert

the musical bells of the cows ambling by
with Mt Shasta floating in the distance

a stalk of lilies, white flowers turning to pink
a small yellow butterfly on the purple asters

and north of White Pass
thirty mountain goats
their whiteness a contrast to the brown scree
above the campsite off the trail at Basin Lake.

Slow down and be still

        and the world unfolds and reveals itself.

        And the gifts are yours.

The View from the Taller Mountain

A cloud
a wisp really
rises up the mountain slope
curves over the top
and following the contour
eases down the other side.

Strange—
I would have thought
that it, untethered,
would just float away
when it had the chance.

Reassurance

The clouds come in
      concealing the mountains.

But I know they are there
      and that's enough.

Written Near Mammoth, California

The constant sound of the wind
in the Ponderosa pines

like the rushing of water through rapids,
the cawing of the nearby raven,

the coolness of the air
that comes with seven thousand feet,

the shimmering winter snows
on the distant Sierra Nevada peaks,

the blue green of the sage,
the yellow green of the pine needles,

and the russet of the tree trunks
heighten my senses as I sit,

coffee in one hand, a book in the other,
my dog curled asleep nearby.

All of this is what I have today.

John Clare, Thoreau, Muir and so many others
      knew about such wealth   and tried to teach us.

Transcendence

Slipping away
are the day's concerns
and yesterday's problems,
displaced by a lone dragonfly,
displaced by an aggrieved chipmunk
its tail synchronized to its warning chatter,
displaced by the nearby sage and pinyon pines,
displaced by distant Mono Lake to the east
and by the mountains of Yosemite to the west.
Even the rumble of cars and motorcycles
ascending Tioga Pass doesn't disturb.

When the transition is made,
possibilities emerge.

On Seeing Eternity in the Distance

The snowy slopes of Mt. Hood rise above the horizon
        seemingly floating above the mountain's dark base
                that blue-grey tree-covered part
                        that fades into the hazy backdrop of the sky.

The clouds touch the snow-capped peak
        claiming it for the heavens
                releasing it from gravity.

Contemplating Time

The moon
        in its last quarter
        is visible
        directly above the summit
        of Mt. Hood
        on this morning
        of the twenty-ninth day of July.

On the north slope
        the snow compacted
        shimmers blue
        in the crevasses.

I wonder,
        am I witnessing
        the birth of a new glacier
        or the death of an old?

The moon has moved off center
but the mountain remains   unchanged to my eye.

The Sixth Extinction

Picture this—
Mount St. Helens looms in the distance
and in the foreground Mt Hood.

Both are silent now but almost forty years ago
Mount St. Helens was over one thousand feet taller
and then abruptly its peak was sliced off.

Forty years and life is returning to the ashy slopes.
First there came the lupines and the fast-growing red alder
though Douglas fir and western hemlock have yet to show.

Red-winged black birds and hawks are back
but very few amphibians.
       The mountain's time is not ours.

We've all seen the pictures
the ashy plumes and the blasted trees
a disaster, the largest eruption in the lower forty-eight,
       nine hours of terror,

though small compared to human-caused destruction
and life will also come back and thrive—
       only we   won't   witness it.

The Pelican Squadron
(or Brief, Pod, Pouch)

The pelicans appear out of the fog
       like ghosts   apparitions   spirits
             not quite there   barely visible   silent.

I hear the waves roiling the sand
I hear the water-rounded pebbles tumbling
I hear the wind fluttering my nylon jacket.

The pelicans appear and disappear into the grayness
      as if they never existed.

Specter-like, another squadron emerges
flying north on this Oregon coast near Langlois,
      a coast with boulders   driftwood   sand
          and a lazing sea lion
the only intruders my dog and I.

Pelicans and a sea lion with the gray ocean and sky,

      the scene feels timeless   and yet . . .

The Flight of the Brown Pelicans

I went for a walk
on the beach today.
The Pacific waves
were coming in high
breaking once
a few hundred feet out
        and then swelling again
                and crashing
      on the pebbled shore.

Brown pelicans,
not the more common white,
flying in a straight line
one behind the other,
approach the smooth face of the wave,
then glide,
        rising as it crests,
                then over to the next,
      soaring the waves
               as hawks do mountains.

I would join them   if I could.

The Oregon Coast Near Langlois

On the beach are
small colorful tumbled stones,
scattered carapaces of crabs,
alien-looking tendrils of kelp,
and soft sand
that makes all walking strenuous.

South are the cliffs
orange and yellow with streaks of red,
cliffs that change as the ocean demands.

North are the dunes
held in place by grasses
with their spidery web of roots,
a last refuge of the Western snowy plover,
and on the leeward side
coyote bush with sweet smelling flowers.

In the distance are the fog-obscured hills
with stunted, lopsided pines
shaped by the incessant wind.

This is the coast near Langlois.

And there a woman walks with a dog,
the fog creating a patina
on her jacket and eyelashes.

There she walks alone
and alone she will be
but for the dog.

Destination Unknown

You've paid for your ticket
now take it and use it.
Let the conductor punch it
or the machine scan it
or the agent collect it.

You don't need to know
          the destination.

You don't need to know
          the route or duration.

You just need
     to pack your bags   and go.

The Unschooled Birdwatcher

There it is again
a reddish brown hummingbird
the whir of its wings announces it.
My personal tick list would be high.
I've traveled the world,
been to beaches and grasslands,
mountain tops and canyons,
deserts and rain forests
and quietly sat
absorbed in my surroundings.
But I can only say that
it's a blue and grey bird
or it makes a clicking noise
or those large brown ones
in a meadow near Mt. Lassen
might be cranes.

Still they bring me pleasure
but I would see more if I knew more.
And now in the mountains near the Rogue River
is another bird singing to me
a common looking brown bird
but an uncommonly beautiful song.

The Rock Garden

Purple pin cushion
baby's breath, yellow asters
and pink sweet pea—
these are the names that I know
and I bestow them
on these wild flowers
on the Oregon hillside
in the Siskiyou National Forest.

These flowers that emerge
from a jumble of rocks
bulldozed aside for a dirt road
find sustenance and are so beautiful
out of so little.

Breathing the Wild

"The exhilarating effect of breathing the wild."
—Nathaniel Hawthorne, *The Scarlet Letter*

You almost don't want to breathe
as if breathing could disturb everything,
disturb the lodgepole pines and Douglas firs,
disturb the aspens with their white trunks and trembling leaves,
disturb the alpine meadow and the scattered patches of snow,
even disturb the sky with its blue deepened by altitude
and beneath that blue the white yarrow, the red poppies
and the yellow and purple of others.
You don't want to breathe
as if breathing could upset the balance
but then you want to absorb it all
so you breathe deeply.

Mountains and Pine Forests

I

In the Idaho mountains near Silver City
exposed rock
resembling the backs of dragons
mark the mountain ridges,
and on the steep slopes
purple stalks of lupine
orange-red Indian paint brush
purple asters
and white and yellow of unknown others
struggle unaware.

    Noticing all
    but unnoticed
    a woman hikes with a dog.

II

The ten-thousand-foot peaks of the Sisters
are glimpsed through ponderosa pines
with red-brown trunks etched with black,
the ground hidden by needles and cones,
their scent released by the sun's warmth.
Manzanita with waxy green leaves
satiny bark the color of cinnamon
other shrubs resembling sage
but not sage
find life below the pines.

> Grateful
> for the shadows
> and the stillness
> of the forest,
> she does not move.

The Amplitude of the Earth

From "Kosmos" by Walt Whitman

All the good words are taken.
I can't string two together
without falling into cliches.
What does the wind do
but caress my skin?
What about the babbling brook
the murmuring of bees
the twittering of birds?
How can I write about this place
with its majestic peaks
the cool mountain air
the spring flowers in August
the velvet carpet of grass,
and even the twang of mosquitos?
How can I write about this place
and not repeat the others?

Here in Eagle Cap Wilderness
I am tongue-tied.
There's something about the sublime
as Wordsworth knew
that humbles and mesmerizes
that sends me searching for words
the way Remington or Frederic Church
reached for paint.

A Visitor to the Night World

At twilight this summer eve
in the sage-dotted desert
north of Shoshone,
two owls hunt
      circling, gliding
         ten feet off the ground,
         soundless with their soft feathers,
one diving at a rabbit
      but veering off.

As I watch not moving,
they fly near,
sometimes directly at me
and I can see into their deep eyes.

By being still   I honor them

         and they   by hunting   honor me.

Fly Fishing

Two entrepreneurs
with colorful plaid shirts
buttoned over their girth—
fly fishermen for the weekend—
stand in a dory
maneuvered by a hired guide
who wades in the fifty-five-degree current.

No graceful arches of line,
but flat slaps against the water,
no gentle landing of cutthroat trout,
but snapped lines
and tangles in the lodgepole pines
should the guide in his boredom
move too close to the bank.

Do they notice
        the emerald green water
                of Henry's Fork
                        as it flows through the canyon
                                with its walls of volcanic rock?

Do they notice
        the bald eagle overhead
                also fishing,
                        or the grey heron
                                motionless on the bank?

Earlier I had seen another angler
        dressed in beige and grey
                sitting on a boulder
                        bent over tying a fly,
                                back rounded like the river rocks.
Twice I looked   before I could see him clearly.

The Rabbits of Coeur d'Alene

There's a rumor that the first was a pet
and the rabbit being a rabbit escaped
another rabbit bought
and   it also hopped away.

And now   and now
rabbits on every corner   on every lawn
front lawn   side lawn   backyard.
Mornings and evenings they congregate
near the hawthorn   near the tulips   near the chard.

Three here   ten over there
the rabbits keep munching
in front of Victorian houses
that sell at highly inflated prices.

One neighbor hand-feeds them
another, not so enamored, trapped twenty
depositing them in the national forest,
the home of coyotes and bears
and probably wolves.

And still there are more
brown, black, white, black and white,
seemingly unaware of dogs and cats.

Capistrano has swallows
Yellowstone has buffalo
Carlsbad has bats
Baja has whales
Tasmania has wombats and quolls,
and Coeur d'Alene   has   rabbits.

Sumptuous Solitude

From Emily Dickinson, poem 1495

I hate to go to sleep at night
here where the stars and the non-twinkling planets
and the gibbous moon light the desert grasses—
     fescue, sedge, wheatgrass, and wildrye—
          their goldness covering the surrounding hills.

I hate to go to sleep at night
here where the silence is all encompassing,
     undisturbed by planes, cars, and trucks
          undisturbed by the chirps and beeps of the tech-driven life.

I hate to go to sleep at night here in this place
that's far away from the frenzy of the news,
     far away from Facebook, Twitter, and Instagram
     far away from email and texts,
     far away from the world of sound and busyness.

Away from it all I hate to go to sleep at night,
I want to stay   immersed   in this Idaho desert night.

The Butterflies of the Amazon

I'm somewhere east of Boise
in the dry-grassed foothills
but I want to talk about the Amazon,
the river basin, not that looming business.
It was the Amazon, wasn't it,
where that butterfly lived.

So here goes—
somewhere in the Amazon
a butterfly flaps its wings
furiously, madly, energetically, ceaselessly
but still that huckster was elected
and now defying all reason
he's re-elected president.

The butterfly tried
so let's not blame that butterfly
and certainly not ourselves,
        let's not blame ourselves.

Ode to Cowboys

There are real cowboys in the twenty-first century
even in this age of greed and corruption,
in this land of the unhealthy.

There are real cowboys who wear wide-brimmed hats
bandannas, slim-fitting jeans,
real cowboys who carry the lingering smell of horses,

who can read the clouds and the wind
and who don't get lost.
There are real cowboys who round up cattle

with border collies as helpmeets
or who carry supplies to camps,
leading a string of pack horses,

cowboys whose ease in a saddle is evident,
cowboys whose bodies are lithe and fit.
These are the people who can be alone

without the chatter of technology or the guidance of GPS
who can survive a storm, freezing rain
who can bear being hungry or tired or wet or cold.

I know I'm romanticizing them

                        but can't we all use a little of that now?

Vedauwoo, Wyoming

Some ashes,
a few small charred pieces of wood
are all that remain
by the granite rocks
where campers had built a small fire,

nothing much remains really
but still an iridescent hummingbird
which usually visits orange and red
searches these ashes
with its long beak.

Hovering inches from the ground
it probes,
        finding something
                where nothing seems to be.

Where the Buffalo Roam

The gentle breathing of buffalo
resembles peaceful snoring
arising out of an echo chamber
or water bubbles being blown in a pitcher.

The soothing low-pitched sound
emanates from the extended family
of massive bulls, cows and the young.
The hum is constant,

but there is also the slurping sound
of the light-colored calves
who follow their suckling
by a hard nudge, bringing more milk.

And there are the sounds of the dominant bulls
sniffing possible mates
and intimidating youthful challengers
but not the white birds that alight on their backs.

The Tetons change color as the sun shifts
but the hum is constant   connecting the herd.

The Kennebec Pass Near Durango

The rocky cliffs of the San Juan Mountains tell a story
        of an ancient inland sea
        of deposited sand and silt
        of the formation of sedimentary rock
        of the rise of the earth's crust
        of volcanoes and glaciers
        of trauma and stress.

The rocks of the pass
        are cracked
        forming small blocks
        precariously balanced.

Some are held in place
        by the roots of Douglas firs
        and some are fissured
        by the same roots.

Fractured the rocks are   but still they resist gravity.

The Beauty of Indirection

On this sparkling day in January
a few snowflakes
float randomly through the air
milling around absentmindedly,
ascending more than descending.
They can't seem to decide on their direction
or even their destination.
Gravity has no hold on them.

They are beautiful in their freshness

                                    much like the youth I know.

Magical Realism Comes to the Desert

With unexpected rain
in southwest Colorado
near the hamlet of Dove
the mundane gives way to the magical
and there it is
a pink horse

       glorious in its pinkness,
       a horse which might once have been white

       before it rolled in the red earth
       but only might have been,

one can't ever be sure.

Sunset at Burnt Ridge

Resembling yellow daisies,
the mules-ears
cover the meadow.
All white columbines,
not the common purple ones,
mark the edge of the forest
filled with white trunks of aspens
that suggest marble columns.

But it's the sunset that amazes.
The colors of Monet tint
the valley and mesas and mountains—
Sleeping Ute, Mesa Verde, and Shiprock.
In the distance a storm lingers
with its timpani roll of thunder,
with its misty streaks
reaching for the desert.

Slowly oranges replace pinks,
gray wisps of rain become apricot
and mauve darkens to purple.
And as if on cue
the coyotes celebrate
the transformation of day to night.

The thirteenth-century cliff dwellers
      were here before me
      and before them
there were the Basket Makers
      and before them
          there were others.

Against Shale Oil Exploration in the Desert

Last year
drought decimated
the cholla and sage and pinyon pines
so this year
shriveled cacti
and dry skeletons of sage
dot the mesa and mountain sides.
Brown needles of pinyons
signal a battle lost,
these hundred-year-old pines
defeated by dryness
and opportunistic beetles.

But May thunderstorms
encourage sprouts
from roots of plants
that crumbled to the touch
twelve months ago.
Dwarf evening-primrose
sego lilies
and spreading daisies
add color to the high desert.
New shoots of sage
begin at the base of the old
and the few surviving cholla and pinyons
seed the next generations.

Homage to Beauty

In the Sangre de Cristo Mountains
at ten thousand feet
there is a small alpine meadow
of only a few acres
with a stream flowing through it.
If you're still
you can hear the water
move over rocks
and if you're really still
you'll see elk at dawn
grazing in the meadow
with its many shades of green
punctuated by patches
of sunny yellow flowers
each with hundreds
of delicate petals.

Botanists call them
by a Latin name—
we call them   dandelions.

The Dance of the Elk

In a small alpine meadow
near Picuris Peak
fifteen miles south of Taos
seven elk graze
on lush May grasses
in the predawn light.
As if by a signal
the elk begin a dance.

One charges
       and the confronted
              meets the challenge
       with a few forward steps,
              then pauses and faces away.

Another charges
       and the ballet continues
              until a circle is formed.

Then as if by another signal
       they disappear
              into the woods of pine—

all of this before sunrise.

Another Dance

Near Rio Chama are cliffs
of muted golds and reds,
home to ravens
so black all color is absorbed.

Sometimes two float from a tree
or the sides of the cliffs.
Flying in unison, they gain altitude
then glide and bank into a turn
supported by unseen air currents.

Then for a brief moment
the ravens face each other
and perhaps touch,
initiating a short tumble,
then they repeat the dance.

        Must there be a choreographer?

Requiem for the Bees

The bees are still here
    in these Colorado mountains.

The bees are still here
    finding the yellow flowers
        that decorate the grasses in the meadow
            bordered by aspen and spruce.

The bees are still here
    and the buzzing reaches my ears
        mingled with the sound of the wind in the trees.

The bees are still here
    amid the flowers and grasses,
        plants untouched by pesticides and herbicides
            uncontaminated by genetic modification.

The bees are still here in the cool mountain air
    and so are the butterflies—
        painted ladies and black swallowtails.

Unlike my home in Alabama
where in my yard planted with jasmine,
both Confederate and North Carolina,

planted with three kinds of salvia, gardenias,
yarrow and so much more,
there are no honey bees.

The zucchinis flower gloriously   but bear no fruit.

Once Upon a Time

The dog stares into the near boulders
on this high mesa of rocks and low-growing sage,
colors of muted grey-green and dusty brown,
the sage smell pervasive
and over all a faded blue sky.

In the distance far below the plateau,
a river adds bright green to the valley.
The dog stills and listens
with patience not often seen
in a heeler-catahoula mix.

She waits for some movement, a smell, a sound
that would signal a furred creature,
a predator hunting.

Once upon a time
our ancestors, those hunter-gatherers,
must have done this.
They knew how to be still,
      how to wait,
           how to see clearly—
traits we have lost.

The dog watches the rocks,
waiting for a sign of a chipmunk
or a rock squirrel with its spotted coat
the color of the earth.

She watches, an unmoving statue,
but then a slight lifting of the head
a refocusing of the eyes
and then the explosion   as she lunges into the sage.

Losing Paradise

There are water hyacinths   clogging southern lakes and rivers,
kudzu   crawling over seven million acres.
zebra mussels   infesting the Great Lakes,
tamarisk and Russian thistle   spreading in the West.

All invasive, all disruptive.

And in Wyoming
in the Wind River Range
at Lake Louise, miles from any town

yellow toadflax
    with deep woody roots
    outcompetes native species
    for sunlight and nutrients
Spotted knapweed
    beautiful with its feathery purple petals
    releases a toxin into the soil
    preventing growth of nearby plants
Hounds-tongue
    with its deep red cup flowers
    and burr-like adhesive seeds
    is toxic to horses and cattle
and so many others   disrupt the balance
dislodge the rightful heirs.

And our contribution—
    hills denuded of timber
    prairies plowed into corn fields
    mountains ravaged by mining
    salmon runs lost to dams.

                more disruption   and destruction.

Mountains and Trees and Caterpillars

In the Manzano Mountains of New Mexico
dense with ponderosa pines and Douglas fir
and bigtooth maples, leaves now scarlet and gold,
a caterpillar, strikingly chartreuse,
with thin black stripes along its length
and bands of green tufts circling the body
tufts with poisonous spikes,
this caterpillar   undulates   along a grey rock.

On this mid September day
the green caterpillar senses a change
      the air is cooler, the days are shorter
      and it knows.
It knows
      the days of nibbling and munching
      the leaves of Gambel oak saplings
      are nearing an end.
It knows
      to spin a cocoon
      and wait
      slowing transforming
      into a zephyr eyed silkmoth.

And we also know things—
      how to destroy cities with our weapons
      how to melt the glaciers
      how to acidify the oceans.

We can even raise the temperature of the earth
a feat   never before   imagined.

But we can't create   one   green   caterpillar.

Our Legacy

What do I have to do this morning
    but drink my coffee and eat a bagel?
What do I have to do
    but watch the chipmunks
    scurry around searching for seeds?
What do I have to do
    but look out over the sage-covered mesa
    alive with doves, ravens, and Western bluebirds,
    the same mesa that harbors a rare milk vetch?
What do I have to do
    but gaze at the red granite boulders and cliffs
    and the snowy peaks of Crested Butte beyond?

What do I have to do
    or maybe the question is
what can I do to save all this
    for my grandchildren
    and their grandchildren.
What can I do?

In the Footsteps of the Dinosaurs

Dinosaurs had almost two-hundred million years
before that fateful asteroid kicked up dust and ash,
blocking the sun's radiation,
dooming those giants.

Our primate ancestors, those that pioneered walking on two legs
appeared maybe four million years ago
and 200,000 years ago Homo Sapiens showed up.

We are so young, babies really,
and we are already doomed
doomed by our own arrogance.

After the fires rage in New Mexico, California, and elsewhere
      after the pine beetles decimate the Colorado forests,
           after the Arctic melts and the seas rise,
                after the droughts and super storms
                      after the earth can't sustain us,
we will join the dinosaurs.

But somewhere, somehow life will continue.
And maybe the next time the evolved creatures
will recognize the gift they were given.

Out of the Ashes Emerge Saplings

After the fires—

      fires started by lightning strikes
      or a careless camper,
      fires worsened by drought,

      some blazes left to burn and smolder
      some combated by chemical-dropping DC-10s
      some attacked by smokejumpers.

After the fires—

      fires that caused road closures and evacuations
      fires that burned houses and towns—
      the Dixie fire consuming 900,000 acres,
      consuming the town of Greenville,

      the Camp Fire destroying Paradise,
      the Mt. Adams fire, the Stehekin fire
      and so many others   too numerous to list,

      fires   that caused   devastation.

After the fires—

    first bare ground   blackened trunks   erosion.

    Within a season sprout the fire follower flowers—
    purple fireweed vibrant against charred pines
    red poppies and paintbrush, yellow arnica, white fire lilies,
    the startling green grasses and ferns—

    all born of fire.

After the fires—

    the knobcone pines of Oregon
    the sequoias of California
    release their seeds   the blazes necessary.

    In a hundred years   a mature forest
    if drought persists   then a meadow.

After the fires—

    renewal and regeneration
        when nature's   given   a chance.

Finding the Magic

The water sparkles and shimmers
in the sudden onslaught of a breeze
that ruffles the surface
of the far shore of Mill Lake,
this high-altitude alpine lake
north of the Colorado village of Ohio City
population sixty-two.

                            There is magic in the world.

Two butterflies search for nectar
visiting yellow flowers,
perhaps dwarf golden asters,
and pause to greet each other,

a dragonfly darts by,
wings gossamer and body iridescent blue,

even the brown back of a fly
shines gold in the sunlight.

                           There is still magic in the world.

The breeze strengthens
all the lake glitters
like the Milky Way,
like diamonds,
like snow and ice crystals.

Slow down   and be still   and the magic is yours.

About the Author

Barbara Wiedemann, professor emerita of English and the former Director of Creative Writing at Auburn University Montgomery, is the author of a critical study, *Josephine Herbst's Short Fiction: A Window to Her Life and Times* (Susquehanna University Press), and four chapbooks: *Half-Life of Love* (2008), *Sometime in October* (2010), *Death of a Pope and Other Poems* (2013), and *Desert Meditations* (2018), all published by Finishing Line Press. Her poetry has been nominated for a Pushcart Prize.

Growing up in the Finger Lakes region of New York with no near neighbors, Wiedemann spent hours roaming the hills, experiences likely forming the basis for her life-long affinity to nature. In recent years, escaping the summer heat and humidity of Alabama, she travels to the mountains of the West where she camps in her van on public lands, her companion an energetic and often out-of-control blue heeler mix. She has hiked the Pacific Crest Trail, beginning at the Mexican border and ending five months later in Washington, and also the Colorado Trail, shorter but just as beautiful. There are days spent kayaking or mountain biking or watching the clouds move along the mountain tops. These experiences have served as catalysts for many of her poems.

www.ingramcontent.com/pod-product-compliance
Lightning Source LLC
Chambersburg PA
CBHW030909170426
43193CB00009BA/784